Whispers
From The Moon

Whispers
From The Moon

A poetry book
By

Lee Broda

ISBN 978-0-578-41839-1

Cover design twinbrush.co.uk

To my family, being away from you is bearable only because I get to do what I love each day. Your endless love and support gives me wings to fly and keep dreaming. I am so blessed to have you. I don't say it often enough, but I love you more than you will ever know. My wish is to make you proud. תודה

To Jennifer Rountree, your classes have been daily gifts that I will cherish forever. Your love for words is contagious, and because of the deep passion you have for language, I discovered the beauty of poetry. I'm grateful to know you and to have learned from you.

Creating a book takes a village, and this book has been nurtured by so many warm and loving hands. Thank you, Castille Landon and Betzi Richardson. Your knowledge and creativity helped shape this book into what it is today. You helped me breathe life into the story these words tell, and doing it without you would have been impossible. Thank you for not allowing me to compromise, and thank you for making sure my vision was always honored throughout this journey.

And finally, thank you, my dear readers, for inviting me to enter your homes and your hearts by picking up this book. Sharing these poems with you means so much to me. Writing *Whispers From The Moon* has helped me heal. I hope that reading it does the same for you. I invite you to share these words with others who may find them inspiring or helpful.

Yours,
Lee

After five years of simply writing to myself in notebook after notebook — collecting piles of colorful words hidden in boxes and drawers, I had to set free the thoughts I'd buried. By pouring these thoughts to paper, I became an explorer of my own mind and heart, and I discovered a way to release pain without falling into it.

Whispers From The Moon is the journey of finding my own voice and the courage to share it with the world.

My wish for the reader of this book is for her to know that she is never alone in suffering or in joy. My wish for him is to explore the deep, hidden edges of his heart between the wandering words of my soul.

Contents

FULL

full

the language of love

I wish I could caress you with language
and do it so well,
it would make you
tremble;
thick, sticky words, touching you
down to your core,
move you,
like music,
sweet melody,
raw honey-
dripping down your lips,
capturing you
the way bees
are drawn to flowers,
circling, buzzing
under nature's spell

you will yearn for me

textile

seven billion human beings wander this planet,
the place we collectively call home,
seven billion combinations of names, cultures, faces,
all afraid of being exposed

we are strangers to each other;
no one cares to know:
what does your heart long for?
what's inside your soul?

and then there's you, who I see so clearly
behind those masks and carefully constructed walls—
I feel you with every sense,
unstitching your fears, hemming your judgments,
weaving the world a new fabric

good morning

The day's first rays leak through our window,
interlaced with the dark,
I can see his serene face,
resting on feather-packed pillows,
breathe in the familiar familiarity of his scent,
filling my lungs with his calmness,
as if capturing it could make it last forever

I inch myself closer to him,
my nose brushes against his prickly beard
my skin kisses his,
warming my fingertips
on the love he emits.
I feel safer between his arms,
even though I'm hollow

coffee

can you take me
dark, bitter, spicy,
but sometimes sweet?
on the days I don't
look, feel, or smell
like me?

can you take me
when I'm smooth,
my aroma delicious,
my taste awakening
every part of you—
an insatiable craving
for me,
for more.

I can be hot or icy,
I can be only yours
to hold,
if you can have me
whole—
at my best,
at my blandest,
at those times
I don't come with cream
to balance the palate

not easy to swallow,
not easy to handle,
but temping
enough
that you'll keep coming back

the one I deserve,
the one I need,
loves me
even when he longs for
tea.

hard rain

we danced outside
while the rain fell hard
on our faces,
happiness stuck
to our lips
when we kissed,
dew drops washed away disagreements

two soaked bodies,
clothes dripping, sticking
to our chests
while dancing
cheek to cheek
on the street
in this crowded place

these little moments are what makes me love you still
and choose you again

and again

     and again

        and

           again

a lion

he says I remind him
of a lion,
especially on the days when
I roar, unsatisfied

maybe my hazel-gold eyes
stare at him so harshly he shrinks,
made half a man, weighted
with unfair expectations and demands

or maybe its my voluminous, unruly hair,
though for years
I tried to fight it, hide it
brushing it violently
coating it in sticky gels,
cutting it too short,
too long,
too dark,
until I let myself be
uncaged,
owning who I am.

you can't tame a lion
(it will turn on you)

the vow

I promise to honor
the woman in me,
even when poison pours from her lips,
searing holes of insecurity
into her beautiful skin

I will embrace her deeply,
even when regret
and past failures
echo
on the walls of her mind

I will love her fully,
even when her heart
shrinks in fear
and shuts me out

I promise to put her first,
heal her wounds of love,
the burn marks on her soul
from far too many disappointments

I will water her with light,
feed her kindness,
kiss her scars,
bathe her with love,

until death do us part

5am

I whisper to the night
a prayer of light,
thanking the moon
for watching over you
during the quiet hours
when I lie in bed
uneasy, alone;
alarming thoughts puncture my sleep,
unwanted worries cling to my body

every night, before the sun breaks through,
small cracks in the blanket of stars
that covers us,
each constellation a night patrol—
standing guard,
singing dreams into your ears,
little lullabies, protecting you
until bright beams of light caress your soft face,
waking you slowly

and we are united again, for a whole day.
my body kisses yours,
morning warmth travels between us;
relieved, you come back to me each morning,
your melting smile, a daily gift;
my sweet
it's hard to let you go
each night

my child

I call out for you
my body feels, it needs you,
even though we haven't met yet

my womb is ready,
warm, spacious, cozy,
though my heart is busy
trying to glue itself back together

I dream of immersing you
with affection
and holding you tight,
never letting go
until you're grown—
I'll never let you go.

I see you so clearly when I close my eyes,
breathing your soft scent, my baby's purity.
I'll cuddle you even after you've said enough—
I'll never let you go.

I never thought
I would be ready
to be a mother,
but now that I'm yours,
never let me go.

keepsake

I weave my darkest secrets
around your wrinkled neck,
into a necklace of colorful dreams,
a rainbow containing all our sorrows and joys,
each bead at peace with the next
my life pressed to your chest,
a silent prayer,
a memory of me to hold

my gratitude to you, mother,
carrying all of our pains
in your dignified way,
the love you have is never-ending,
enough to last until we meet again.
no matter where you go
we are tied together, beads.

a picture book of you

holding you between my trembling hands,
dancing through the pictures of your life,
seeing stories you never told a soul,
hand-written words whisper to me
from each page;
memories of you, for me to carry

I danced until your pages were full of me,
coloring your photos with my tears,
our lives entwined, tangled,
not knowing where you end and I begin

between the pages, empty spaces,
moments erased,
your silence screams.
I wish I could weave you back to life—
I promise I won't shut you down this time,
I will allow you to ask endless questions
(though I still don't have answers)
again and again and again

I will invite you to dance with me,
on our faded pages of the past,
let you live on in them until forever,
pressed tightly
in my heart

my women

drowning us in big bear hugs,
their magic hands cure every cut,
real or imagined, lifting my spirit up,
mysteriously able to do it all,
balancing life,
love,
loss
on the sides of their hips,
working with their hands, thinking nothing of it

but my women aren't celebrated
for their motherly touch;
they are taken for granted,
rarely appreciated.

I wish I could be as selfless as them,
be their benevolent caretaker
as they transition, beginning to fade.
I cherish every moment I get to love them,
following in their footsteps but gifted
the opportunity to explore another path

shabbat

every Friday I kissed his raspy hand
after he placed it on my small head,
wild with curls,
quietly mumbling
a prayer of protection
his eyes closed—
like God took over for a moment—
and, through my grandpa's body,
whispered
you are loved

I miss those chaotic family dinners,
dozens of us gathered around,
the kid's table congested with laughter and yelling,
small Egyptian decorated plates
overflowing with homemade challah braids
and hummus spreads,
a rainbow of colors,
each representing
our history
our family
our past,
       present,
            future
traditions I will pass to my own family,
preserved like Milk and Honey

playing adults

remember those days
when we were bold,
clinging to tree tops,
kings and queens
of our own, imagined castles,
unstoppable

remember those days
we'd wake before dawn to sit outside,
dewy grass tickling our toes,
drinking the world with our fresh eyes,
all obstacles surmountable,
surrounded by possibilities,
a universe without plan B's

remember those days?

possessing an abundance of talent,
but confused:
which path do we choose?
I followed the wrong one.

how did we let those days
slip through our fingers,
our heads lost in the sky,
dusting dirt off our knees

the door to your soul

when God appears at the door of your soul,
open it wide,
let her enter,
fill and expand you.

trust her
to spark your mind,
ignite your fire,
inspire your heart,
and breathe life back into every wounded cell

her magic can heal the lies
you allow to live inside you,
beliefs that poison your thoughts,
destroy your worth,
taint your happiness

trust her;
she is God

paper and plastic

a crowded coffee house, full
of people, heads down, distracted,
searching for meaning
in all the wrong places,
wanting another body to hold at night
instead of the ice-cold touch of devices,
chasing disembodied humans
to heal our brokenness,
as if they'll be the cure-all to loneliness,
as if they'll make us whole again

running after others,
trying tirelessly to impress
but missing the one
sitting right in front of us

just look up

maybe it's the guy nestled in the corner,
his salt and pepper hair buried in a book,
or the one in skinny jeans,
having a conversation
over cup of black coffee

he looks up

in an instant, you can fall in love

a hive

my body is a beehive
seducing you,
unexpected and sweet;
you keep coming back,
wrapped in sticky kisses,
sensual nights
buzzing around me,
until you get what you want ,
until you get what you need,
until you get my honey.

I only see you when you need to be fed.

waning

maybe the moon

goodnight moon, I whisper.
from upstairs, I hear him calling my name,
come to bed!
my worries hang heavy,
clouds above my head;
there is work to be done before morning

words, confusion, fill my mind,
overflowing images of loss and sorrow,
the bitter taste of betrayal blinds my senses,
carves a hole, leaving me naked,
bleeding on the bathroom floor

I can't fight my mind-
I've tried about a thousand times;
raising the white flag,
I surrender to the voice inside.

but those stubborn thoughts follow me
with every step, they hover just behind
when I climb into bed, they crawl beside me,
reclaiming their worn spot
in the silence between the dots

their heavy weight fills the bedroom,
his body buried beneath the sheets,
next to mine;

my mind is racing,
trying to embrace the pain
that mumbles sleepy, destructive words
into the dark night

maybe the moon will know what's right?

the bakery on 2nd St

hand touches hand,
hearts beat fast,
strolling together down
our joint path

cracked grey sidewalk,
a homeless man weeps,
we both move along,
no one speaks

numbed by pain,
the loneliness inside,
a need to feel wanted,
without being left behind;
not wanting to be exposed,
controlled by our fears,
your silence is deafening.

outside, the storm is threatening,
a cold winter morning pulls us in,
a crowded bakery on 2nd St,
the smell of fresh ground coffee
and sugary ginger bread,
the rain washes over
words left unsaid

the way he looks at me

reminds me of a distant memory,
myself, studying my father's adoring gaze
as he watched my mother
while she cooked
in our small, cream-brown kitchen
on Friday mornings, before Shabbat

the way he looks at me
feels familiar,
and I, an open book,
let him read me.
even on those days when I don't recognize myself,
I pretend not to notice,
just like my mother did

If only he was able to love me
the way my father loved her

If only I was able to keep him
looking at me
like that
forever

invisible

am I invisible,
standing next to you,
solid but small,
supporting every step you take,
asking no questions at all.

I am the unseen force
that drives us forward,
fighting battles,
moving mountains,
just for you.

I wish you would chase away my fears
and hold me when I'm low,
knowing now you're no longer capable
of bearing my weight.

I miss the days you used to
cup my melting heart.

I wish you still got me,
like you did at the start.

empty

open fields covered in snow,
the sun reflects off the watery leaves,
rays sparkle, lighting up your face,
even though your eyes
hold tight to your tears

you turned your head
hoping I couldn't see the storm within,
but your shoulders give you away,
hunched with heavy loss,
I can see it in the sides of your
smile, lips curled but too tense,
trying to hold it all together

clouds invade the clear sky,
your mood synced with nature;
its shift releases your emotions,
baby it is ok to feel,
I whisper.
but you won't let me in,
you won't let it out .

crumbs

lost in the woods,
following the crumbs of love
you toss around,
empty words served on a silver tray
blow in the wind
and disappear,
like dust on winter's wings

but chasing crumbs is not enough—
I'm starving;
my empty well
yearns for rain—
I'm thirsty—
for a human touch on my skin,
kisses on my forehead,
a body to hold at night,
to warm my cold sheets

you only ever offer crumbs,
leaving me
alone
in the dark

my ocean

you are my ocean,
calm and steady,
warm glass,
until you turn on me
in sharp swells,
crashing against my sails

a merciless ocean
dragging me under
weighty waves,
your tide rushes in,
drowning me,
with your current expectations

sinking deeper,
until I'm out of reach,
        out of breath,
            out of my own depth
until the person I see is no longer me

whirlpool

a deadly pool of love,
your acid and my anger,
a tear in the line,
leaking tears
of torment,
filtering out every joyful space in my soul

you are the ocean
I chose to bathe in

do we choose love?

I always believed
you had chosen me
from a world full of exceptional options,
you were drawn
inexplicably,
your eyes smiled, gaze set on mine;
my heart recognized its other half,
whispering in rhythmic beats:
he's the one

but my mind objected:
run

pulled in opposite directions,
driven to madness over you,
not sure which side will win

this battle isn't over yet

enemies

how did we become strangers,
chasing a fairy tale
that existed only in our minds,
fantasies that made us blind,
and now all we're able to see
is our fear

boulder

we are trapped in our past,
dragging it into our future,
carrying it on our backs;
with all of our fighting,
it grows heavier,
hanging, a boulder over our lives

two sides

willing to sacrifice each other,
for the sake of being right ,
trying to win a meaningless fight

we are no longer happy

shrinking
into a ball of frustration
about to **explode**,
shooting angry arrows
i n   e v e r y   d i r e c t i o n ,
wanting to melt the walls
we've built between us
two strangers who share a common world
but can't live in the same household

how do you walk
away
from
love?

the end is near

an avalanche crashing
down a steep mountain,
the end is near

we are dragging each other,
tumbling down, bloody scratches,
scars etched on the love we nurtured
and protected for years

the end is near—
this is no fairy tale,
where the princess wins the prince
and lives happily ever
after she kissed so many frogs
along the way
to further failure

scorpion

you are what you think you are,
doesn't matter what I see;
an ink-black Scorpion,
hiding in his armor, from the future self
he doesn't want to be

your claw, wrapped tight around my neck,
suffocates me,
pincers raised at the ready,
prey within your sight,
I can't escape the sting of your love

you always warned me,
Scorpios don't change.

deadly love

my heart pounds, violent,
about to explode,
a ticking bomb,
every beat louder
and faster

I watch it happen over and over,
every word
a thick poison
slicing my chest open
all the way
to my beating heart

my golden cage

your stirring presence
a dangerous whirlpool,
sucks me abruptly inside;
I get caught in the web
of your dark eyes,
your arms a cage
slowly closing in on me,
but my body longs to be free—

and maybe it's time...

destruction

insecurities,
starving one while feeding another,
fueled by destructive words,
an outburst of
alien behaviors flare,
turbulent,
raging on, uncontained

exposed,
I can no longer use them
as second rate excuses,
placing them center stage
while I wait in the wings

when neglected,
dangerous words smolder,
spreading slowly,
leaving debris,
multiplying like wild weeds

this morning

we hugged for an hour,
like holding on could hold us together;
crying, as if tears could clean our slate,
fend off this impossible goodbye,
each of us trying
to force the other
to walk away

I begged you to leave,
weeping as I watched you struggle
to pack your little, blue suitcase,
sitting on my hands
so I wouldn't reach out,
keep you from walking out the door

we both know we shouldn't stay
in this destructive love affair,
but with that glance over your shoulder,
I know I'm too afraid to let you go

cutting ties

my goodbye letter to you,
my lover, my best friend,
written with you next to me in bed,
in secret, before the fall,
seeing the future collide with the past,
cutting the ties now,
knowing they'll never last

how many more nights
can I cry myself to sleep?
burying choked tears in the hard pillow,
protecting you from my pain,
another night of tossing and turning again,
uncertain until the end,
tides ever changing
and I'm always half empty;
is your love enough to fill both of us?

spiders

two naked bodies
laying back to back,
the small space between them
in the shape of the fight
they just had

trapped in their past
a web of dissent is spun,
expanding,
pressed into the sheets,
thickening with each lashing
of angry words,
contaminated blood
coursing through their veins

the web tightens,
threatening to capture them,
crushing
what is left:
two lovers unable to love

dangerous words

words roll off the tip of my tongue,
bounce from my lips into the air,
where they transform, beyond my control,
gaining strength, multiplying in meaning,
until they reach your ears,
where you patiently wait to capture them,
to hold them tight, then rewind,
twisting them, playing each word back
against me,
vines tightening around my throat,
igniting unwanted fires

dangerous words
come between us
and disappear
when needed most

goodbye

rearranging life,
rearranging meanings,
shifting the weight I gave you,
removing you from my being,
entwined souls
unravelled

I'm learning how to leave you,
       how to breathe you out
       from every part of me
       that craves your touch,
       longs for your warmth,
       now abandoned

our bodies will stay thirsty,
yearning
for a broken love.
our story ends here,
with one word
I couldn't say for years—

eclipse

black sheets

his back is turned,
heavy breath,
eyes hard shut,
his warm body swallowed
by the lead black sheets,
(a mountain between us)
barricading him

naked side by side,
vulnerable yet distant,
he hasn't forgiven me since that night,
hanging angry words over my head
every day

his punishment is cruel
yet brilliant;
I surrender all control,
give him the key—
now he can turn me on or off,
play my heart's strings,
operate the gentle machinery
as he wishes
       more
            less
      enough
          stop
    go
         come back

hard wiring confusion into
my system,
a virus I can't destroy or remove.
unable to read his intentions,
I'm left to his mercy,
swallowed nightly by the emptiness
of these cold black sheets

black tar

another tear in our womb of love
crumbling
under the heavy expectations
we heave at each other

whipping words,
lashing out loud,
we are digging our graves

love turned to madness,
black tar
spilling from our lips,
no longer able to stop
the destruction
spread between us

a living nightmare,
I can't wake up;
unable to break free,
nailed to the floor
we cannot move, we cannot choose

two broken bodies holding tight

flags

he served me lies on a silver tray
decorated with his charming betrayals,
handcuffed me with polished promises,
a chain of fancy words, fantasies
tarnished when I confronted him

he served me endless excuses,
pleading for forgiveness,
begging to build a bridge
back over the shaking ground,
a chasm threatening to swallow us

and even though I knew better
I stayed for far too long,
carrying his lies like flags,
evidence of our broken love
blowing in the deceitful winds

a man in disguise

your predatory pupils
dug into mine
while you fed me sweet lies,
serenaded me with delicate words
of deceit

you pretended
you were a rare find,
a gold mine,
you lured me in with promises,
said I could lean on your heart
throughout life,
words that still ring in my ears,
deafening

you were haunted,
terrified of your own shadow
chasing you,
threatening
to reveal the dark secrets
you'd buried,
now suffocating, dying within you

I realize now I never knew the true you,
choosing to believe the delusion that
you were only mine.
now I'm forced to confront
the reality
of losing you

as if she was magic

as if I were her,
as if I wasn't the one
left behind bleeding
without the sparkly fairy tale
he promised, whispered
in my ear again and
again

I dress differently,
disguised in a flowery-citrus scent
that doesn't belong on my body,
but fits her so perfectly
with each spritz, I wish it was me

I stare at her, the way she moves with ease,
floating like a feather
through life,
as if she came out of the womb
knowing how to live so free
and steal men
like magic

bleeding

I live in a divided world
of love and hate,
residue of you

my blood is anger
boiling over,
drops of poison
mark my way
to our broken bed

I crawl back
next to you,
a puddle of misery
staining our sheets.
reopening the wounds
to punish myself
for being weak,
for wanting you back.

visions of you with her pervade
a vicious cycle
of pain
contaminating every layer of my life;
it hits hard,
like bare feet pounding
the hot pavement

end of love

our love is buried
under a pile of heavy
words,
sharp thorns poked holes
in it;
all the air vanished,
it's left an empty, wounded vacuum

only hate surfaces now

weak

one day your heart will be ripped out of your chest
brutally,
        violently,
                unexpectedly
while you stand there, watching from the side line

you allowed it to happen
        slowly,
        surely,
because you were too weak
        to be the first
                to walk away

betrayal

you were the rock,
our solid foundation,
holding me;
your love was my bridge to sanity,
my corner of peace
where I could hide,
shielded
by your arms

but you were the one who broke me,
robbed my trust,
when your lies
were revealed
and the truth
slapped me in the face,
mercilessly

there are no more tears left
to water this burnt heart;
each wave of grief breaks harder,
pulling me under,
drowning me

entranced

his fingers pressed
to my mouth,
body clinging
to mine;
we are wrapped
in each other,
naked, thirsty, needy

I sold my soul
coming back here,
my loneliness
in the guise
of tender affection;
there is no escaping him

his spell is unbreakable

black magic

his spell is unbreakable
and I am a fool
who keeps coming back for more,
his cloying potion
temporarily satisfying my hunger;
the moment my lips touch his skin,
a rush of relief spreads through my veins.
I am an addict
falling for him
immediately,
again and again

struggling to recover,
I am left thirsty
for days on end

happiness

chasing myself in circles,
downing uppers, unable to sit still,
rewinding the moments
when our love felt so real

my sanity's in jeopardy,
slipping through my fingers,
combining cocaine and wine,
a chemical seduction in my mind,
small glimpses of shrinking highs

alone with myself,
always craving more,
hiding my addictions,
I've lost all control.

finding happiness after you
is not so simple after all.

bitter

fear seeps in through the cracks,
congealing into a puddle of dread,
severely wounded and rejected,
a flood of dark emotions
drag me down,
a sink hole of depression,
I can't pull myself out
til the taste on my tongue turns me bitter,
unrecognizable,

how did I get so far from love?

nothing will ever

I struggled to shut the door
on our inferno love,
just before my heart collapsed,
burnt,
turned to ash

I started sleeping
diagonally,
my small, broken body
swallowed by our king bed,
now cold.
even the pillows miss you.

every room echoes your absence;
nothing will ever sound the same,
nothing will ever smell the same:
our sheets
my clothes
my body

all went down in flames.

a puzzle

he doesn't owe me
anything
anymore
now that we are over

how does the heart understand
going from everything to nothing
in one instant?
one moment,
when it all cracks
and you are no longer two but one,
alone again;

from the closest soul in the world
to a stranger

you shattered us
without thinking twice—
our pieces don't fit anymore.

a storm

the door burst open,
tossing your grey sneakers aside,
shutting off all the lights
on your way to me

now I need to keep them on
to help chase away the darkness
of your absence

you'll never leave your brown leather jacket
in the entrance way
anymore
or close all the blinds,
complaining the neighbors
can see us

you aren't coming back this time—
that thought a punch to my stomach,
knocking the air out of my lungs,

windswept in the aftermath

searching for the unattainable

with you I am blind,
yearning to be seen

under every overturned rock,
I find your face
reflecting off the dirt,
mirroring the darkness
you forced on me
the day you disappeared

every empty room in this house we built
echoes your absence
imagine how we could've
taken up arms,
fighting each other's demons

but we are better off apart,
without our judgments standing between us,
time at our throats,
keeping score

furniture

struggling to divide
the pile of life
we collected
throughout these gentle years:

our worn leather couch,
the squeaky wooden bed,
two cream love seats,
the silky sheets that
held all my tears

every time I pass by
the uneven mirror in the hall,
the one you built yourself,
I see our bodies making love

all our belongings are stained
with our love,
with our heartbreaks,
our memories captured
in this house, between these walls,
pressed into the furniture,
a photo album of our lives

sleep

his arms were once the safest place,
his neck the softest,
his chest the most calming,
familiar, welcoming,
where I could fall asleep so easily

sleep...
I haven't slept since that night—
deep, calm, uninterrupted sleep;
instead I'm haunted,
desperate for the shores of unconsciousness,

so I can escape him
for a moment
and pretend everything
didn't end
the day
he left

even the walls cry your name

even the walls cry your name
at night—
they miss you.

they miss the pictures I hid,
the ones that told our story,
shoved into a drawer
with all our memories
that are still alive,
breathing inside of me,
clinging to every cell,
every room still smells of you,
refusing to fade.

this house was once our home,
now it is a stranger—
cold, unfamiliar and distant,
just like you.

a second skin

I've stopped counting the nights
I fall asleep
bathed in my tears

I've become desperate
unsure if I can heal from you,
unsure how I can survive you;
I barricade my heart,
shut the blinds on my soul
from the world I created,
where you are imprinted into
everything I own,
every person I know,
every dress I wear,
every picture hanging on the fridge

I don't know how to remove you
                              from me

you don't belong

I want to lock you away,
leave you behind,
in my past,
without dragging you into my future;

you don't belong there anymore.

home

he is now a stranger
that feels like home,
every time
I see him,
every time
I touch him.

let the right one in

I forgot how tall he was,
his threatening figure standing in the door way.
our eyes meet,
his presence shatters me

he reaches out,
his bare arms
open, inviting,
his red, swollen eyes
begging to be forgiven,
to be understood
but I know he isn't any different

I wish I could wash away
all the mistakes he made,
still smeared on the walls of our past,
in every room of this house

with small, hesitant steps,
I advance
cautiously towards him,
my doubts like sharp knives
poking through

don't let him back in,
I scream to myself silently,
but his skin is tired, cracked,
rough from sleepless nights;
I'm drawn in,
a puppet on strings,

taking in his heavy breaths,
his wet cheeks,
stained with sweat
and tears,
his rapid heartbeats,
like drums in my ears

he wants me to forgive him,
he wishes I was weak like him,
weak enough to let him crawl back in

i'll change

how do you heal
broken promises
of "change",
when all that's left
is pain,
etched on every body part you touched

echo

saturday bells echo in the distance;
even in your absence
I feel your presence
ringing in my ears

your shadow follows me
with every step,

lingering behind me

footsteps of neglect

walking through the house
without a clear purpose
following the cracked, wood floor
spider webs hang from the ceiling
of the dark and chilly room
a window in the back
swings open-shut , open-shut,
gently, with hesitation
almost unnoticed;
it doesn't want to interrupt
the silence of the house

with every step the place comes to life,
echoing the pain it witnessed
the only evidence of the past
marked on the crumbling walls

a strange feeling creeps in
like an unwanted lover
missing pieces everywhere;
all that's left is the wreckage
of a broken
love

water in my lungs

you weren't the one for me,
but imagining you
touching someone else tenderly,
the way you used to touch me,
hurts like being held
under water

the last time

you came home tonight
to return
your key,
the last time
it's just you and me.

this will be the last time we
lock eyes, minds, arms,
skin on skin,
communicating without our lips
uttering a single word.

this will be the last time
you brush my hair,
inhaling me
like a spring day
just after the rain.

this will be the last time
we share a meal,
we share our day,
we share a bed,
we need to stop.

your eyes search for mine,
pleading for one more
moment before
we have to say goodbye;
I look away
so I can pick myself up
when you leave

you left the key behind,
along with your heart.

waxing

forgiveness

I learned how to live with forgiveness,
how to let go of the pain
that came with loving you,
how to let go of the idea
of not having you
anymore

painting over the images of us in my mind,
removing you
from each frame,
peeling you off my heart,

forgiving you for everything you aren't,

forgiving myself for waiting
for you to become it
one day.

bewitched

he cast a silent spell on me,
held by his hexing charm,
forever stuck in his web, a prisoner
feeding on small crumbs of affection,
offered with nonchalance

his hold on me was terrifying;
I shrunk a size
to fit his expectations,
to win a sliver of appreciation
that never came

I was lost,
blind,
feeling my way in the dark,
searching for an opening,
an escape
from the jail of his manipulative magic

my soft whimpers from behind the bars
transformed into loud prayers,
stronger than his curse;
my voice came back to me,
demanding to be free

I will never let a man have a hold on me this way, ever again.

my heart's whispers

for years my heart whispered
the answers I was seeking;
they came and went like the wind,
sometimes
small, quiet, soft,
during the day;
sometimes loud as thunder
in my prophetic dreams,
during the night,
wrapped around my body
when I lay in bed,
resting right before my eyes,
but I refused to see,
I refused to listen

instead I chose to ignore
their tangled meanings,
intimidated by the unknown.
the lonely path my heart suggested
was filled with landmines and thorns,

so I stayed
in the mud and the madness
for another year,

until the truth caught me like a deer,
slammed into me
and forever changed me.

I will never ignore again
when the heart whispers—
leave.

time

I never paid attention to the seconds
I took for granted,
all the brief, passing moments
I had with him:

when our eyes locked
across the room,
sharing a judgment about someone;
when our lips touched
and we pressed into each other,
when his big hands caressed my messy hair
even though I always asked him to stop

our life together was made
of those fleeting seconds,
minutes, hours
pieced together,
moments I will never get back

they trickle down,
sand,
passing through me,
fading from my memory,
from my body,
while I try to hold on to them
before they escape,
betraying me

just like him

until forever

a distant memory
suppressed,
emerges with the copper flame
of that autumn-crisp candle,
the last birthday gift
I ever got to give you

every time I light life into it,
its aroma brings you back,
your warmth tickles
the cold air
of an early winter morning
in our disheveled home

a lonely flame,
I wait for you in silence,
still too proud to beg,
burying my soft whispers
in letters you will never read
wishing you would come back and love me

mourning

I've been mourning us
since our first fight,
foreseeing the scene of our breakup
playing in a tormenting loop:

you saying goodbye,
saying you're sorry,
you'll never be enough.

I always knew you'd take the coward's way out.

and me sitting on our bed,
rolled into a ball of sorrow,
grieving for days,
a moon chasing a sun chasing a moon,

collecting my wounded heart,
all the broken pieces,
washing the blood off the floor
with my tears.

I had a year of practice, rehearsing,
but the day you left
still shattered me.

I wasn't sure how to heal from you.

some mornings

it's been months since we broke each other,
and I'm still struggling to smile,

cast away hard wonders;
what might have been's?
interrupt my daily tasks,
even the easy ones

like waking each morning,
brushing my teeth,
putting the kettle on to make ginger tea
without me boiling over

soften

I used to feel invincible;
nothing could crack me
people, death,
disappointments,
none succeeded in unseating me

my heavy shield of fear
maintained a safe divide
between the enemy
and me,
so impenetrable
not even love could break through

so I set down my shield,
stepped out of my armor;
unprotected, I fought to change,
learning how to soften.
vulnerability, like bullets,
was unbearable,
but opened the door,
letting my soft, feminine self
shine;

for men to walk in
and visit,
even if only for a brief night

this constant battle between
fearing and wanting love
still rages inside,
threatens me
daily

cemetery

dreams buried
turn to dust,
each passing day
digging us deeper,
trapping us
in graves of unfulfilled
desires
we avoid and dance around
our entire lives

suffocated by
secret passions,
choked by
the leaden hands of others' demands;
giving up
is an open wound

whispers carried on howling winds
begging you, try again,
small signs the universe
sends your way,
daring you to start anew

second best

I didn't come into this world to be silver or bronze,
to be your second choice,
or even to win
the *honor* of being loved by you

my heart on autopilot,
set to give, give, give,
and you just keep on taking,
never taking me into consideration,
leaving me off the podium

if practice makes perfect,
with you I deserve first,
but I always end up sweeping the bottom
of your priority list

my rock bottom

my rock bottom gave me hope
while you left me bleeding,
hanging;
I will never let you in again.
I know better,

even if you've changed.

moving on

I learned how to be at peace with loss,
how to wake up every morning
without looking for you,
how to end each day
without calling you,
how to sleep in our bed again,
alone,
peacefully, through the night

my body feels like mine again,
so does my face,
so does my mind;
my bones don't ache for you anymore

I stopped praying you would come back
and we could act
like nothing has changed
between us,

like I wasn't in a battlefield
for months,
not eating, not sleeping,
fighting through the tears,
crying you out
of my body

so sure my heart
was missing
a piece
skipping a beat
each time I saw your name
on my screen

thank god you don't call anymore

rain

waiting for you
to wash him away,
remove his scent from my skin,
cleanse me

only you can water my sapling heart,
thirsty for your comfort,
your inviting touch
to caress my face,
to drown me in calmness,
each drop
a storm in my veins

stuck in this desert,
pleading with the sun
for your arrival,
but you are an oasis,
always ten steps away

chasing you around the world
to reunite,
your small, clear pearls
revive me

I pray for you
to arrive;
it's already November—
I pray
but you aren't here
(yet)

rainbows

a rainbow of scars
mixed with fresh memories
are tattooed on my body;
I've collected the clutter,
pain piled on my shoulders,
the weight of which
leaks into my heart

it grows heavier,
needy,
inked and linked
to every new love,
still shackled to me,
not wanting to part
and be forgotten
with time

fading disco ball

and you will find me
underneath the disco ball
dancing, fierce,
mourning your absence
with every song that plays,
collecting pieces of my brokenness,

shedding my memories of you,
second skin I no longer need,
your shadow fading in the distance,
finally able to erase your image

I am wrapped in loneliness,
                                        and I am free.

the edge

standing on the edge,
looking ahead,
my fantasy future floating
calmly in front of me

if only I could reach out
and grab it,
make it my own;
this illusion
a cruel game
my mind plays
repeatedly

is it really mine to hold?
always a step ahead,
I am forever trying to catch up,
chasing it
in circles,
my tail tickling my nose,
almost touching it

goodnight

I keep sparks of sunshine
under my pillow
to brighten up
my lonely nights,
to keep me company
when the clouds
steal the stars,
capture the moon,
darken my dreams,
casting shadows in
my cold bedroom, allowing
my secrets to run free
with the warm winds
of early July

(I keep them under my pillow
to protect me from me)

time to say goodbye

lying on the twin bed
in my childhood home,
memories flood my mind:
familiar smells of warm cake
sneak up on me,
the past all too present
in this moment—
nothing has changed
except me

twelve years older,
my body slightly shifted,
new wrinkles around my eyes
no one will ever recognize
except me

missing my dreaming self
from the last decade,
afraid to wake
old insecurities, dropped,
though they accompanied me
keeping me safe,
a shield from myself.
I no longer need protection.

us

we are equal,
all the same,
except when we aren't,
and then who can we blame?

we think we are different
when we're really just the same,
living in an endless circle
chasing money, chasing fame

but humanity is in jeopardy,
selfishness a rising tide,
sinking, silent, unable to see
the needs of the other side

Time's up, it's time to stand up
for ourselves and something bigger
even when we're filled with fear

because time is running out—
our life is slowly slipping away,
waiting for change to come;
if not now, when?

and still we rise

we rise from the ashes,
our voices ripple in the field;
one brave soul stands to stutter out her history,
beads of sweat roll-down her silenced cheeks,
recounting the years of being struck
by a man she once loved—
roll up your sleeves , it's not over yet

dreams of sorrow echo ahead,
another woman buried,
her pain and death left unexplained,
her dreams locked in her lifeless heart—
roll up your sleeves , it's not over yet

women come together,
gather by the creek
to be heard, to rise together,
to finally feel complete

roll up your sleeves,
though you are afraid
speak all that has been left unsaid,
stuffed down, forcefully forgotten,
and still you will rise

tribe

I am brave,
braver than before,
shifting,
a sheep into a lion,
evolving into a great warrior

I am a fighter,
stronger than before
molding
flesh into metal,
becoming my own protector

I'm an extension of all women,
each a part of my history,
a tribe older than life,
running through my veins;
our voices will always surface,
echoing out from the dead

treasures of the universe

the blood moon smiled at me
with its bright red beams
reassuring me of its presence

the waves washed
my sandy toes,
warmed my body.
the wind filled my pockets with ocean breeze,
wove sea shells into my hair,
a woman made beautiful
by specks of moon light

facing north

a brown leather couch,
open windows facing north,
bright sun warms the room,
rays illuminating the empty, worn spot
beside me, reminding me where he once sat—
just there,
I could reach out
and touch his hand
if I wanted,
but I never dared.
now it's just me
and the sun
in this cold, empty room,
facing north

new words

there are so many words
I want to share with you,
new words my body never felt before;
I want to draw them on your lips,
whisper them to you
while you fall asleep
and part with the day
slowly,
next to me

mellifluous words to calm your spirit,
witty words to challenge your mind,
lustful words to feed your hungry soul,
to bridge the distance between
you and me

words pulled us apart
and words will bring us together
one day,
when our two worlds will speak
the same language—
love

About the Author

Lee Broda is an Israeli-born poet who writes about the beauties - and uncertainties - of life from a distinctly observant perspective. Lee's love for poetry and writing began when she was a teenager, growing up in rural Israel.

As a celebrated actor and producer, Lee's intelligent and passionate creative drive is known globally. Significantly, as founder of LB Entertainment, which develops, finances, and produces major independent films, she has shepherded over thirty films to success.

LB's films have premiered at the world's top film festivals, and have been distributed worldwide, garnering international recognition, and numerous awards.

Additionally, Lee is the founder of Women Creating Change, an organization that bridges, empowers, and creates opportunities for female writers, directors, producers, and actors from the Middle East.

To date Lee has kept her poetry private; *Whispers From The Moon* is her first published collection which she proudly shares now.

About the Book

Whispers From The Moon is a collection of poetry about
love
loss
grief
heartache
and the empowering of oneself, triumphing over all to
celebrate the beauty of life.

It is divided into four chapters corresponding to the
phases of the moon: full, waning, eclipse, waxing.

The book is a companion to all of us in our life's journeys,
encouraging us to live authentically with passion,
acceptance, forgiveness, and ultimately, love.

Please join me at www.leebroda.com.

I would love to hear from you, and to be able to keep you up-to-date about my book signings and media events.

Thank you for taking this journey with me.

Made in the USA
Monee, IL
15 October 2021

80113357R00074